White Tights Black Lights

Chloe Chaotic

Presentation by *BookLeaf Publishing*

Web: www.bookleafpub.com

E-mail: info@bookleafpub.com

ISBN: 9789357444101

First edition 2022

Weeping Willow

Sylvia's silver in the moonlight
A blood moon eclipse in Taurus
An omnipresent willow tree
O Willow Waley
As she weeps and wails Pearly-Dewdrops drop
Plump as figs that one day will rot
Sat in the crotch of an omnipresent willow tree
O Willow Waley-
Give me back my baby

Christmas Carol

Carol in gold enamel
Glossed red nails clicking on a mirrored surface
Mirrored like the glaze of big sad eyes
Haunting ghostly cries
Compacts that click and snap
Wonderland oyster aphrodisiac
Carol in gold enamel
A candle-lit midnight mass
Her heels echoing on the stone floor
Her hair doesn't sit curled so softly anymore
Compacts that click and snap
Pearls with a clasp back-
Sometimes her arms bend back

White Tights

The black dahlia
Bruised violets
White roses painted red
My flower bed
Lichen
Moss
White tights stained green
Porcelina figurine-
The realm of soft delusions, floating on the
leaves

Black Lights

Fluorescein
Black lights
Tangerine Dreams
Strange nights
Fluorescein
Black lights
Crime scenes
Parasites

The Wheel Turns

Weaving in and out of love like plaits in golden
hair-
Or a Maypole dancer
At a Beltane Fayre
By Autumn come it's all undone
By Winter there's another one

Rotten Fruit

The sky hung with jewels in the black night
His hair lay in a basket that's been set alight
He is cut from forehead to belly and eaten raw
In a nettle bed of thorns on the woodland floor
Rotten fruit falls and festers with time-
Karmic sweetness like cherry wine

The Two-Headed Calf In Heaven

Every sky goddess and deity
Aura, Aurae-
Will love him beyond comprehension
A Taurus Son, Gemini Ascending to Heaven
Until his mother arrives there too

Tomino's Hell

It's going to be a fine night tonight
It's going to be a fine day tomorrow
Tears in the eyes of cute Tomino
It's going to be a fine night tonight
It's going to be a fine day tomorrow
The lonely journey of cute Tomino
Dragged to the bottom of a well
Dragged through Tomino's hell
Wet black hair emerging through a TV-
If they're in Hell bring them to me

Spiderwebs

A thin sprawling veil spun gladly-
Roses into gold
Lilac into honey
Everyday is alchemy

Heaven And Nature

The maiden, The mother, The crone
The triple goddess
The Divine Feminine
Heaven and nature sing

The Unholy Trinity

The all seeing eye
Unholy Trinity
Wild eyed
Furrowed brow divinity

12-02-1999

1 Gemini Ascendant
Deflection by way of comedy
The mask worn
Ruler of duality
6 Scorpio Mars
Soul tie intensity
Devotion
Mystery
7 Sagittarius Pluto
Karmic energy
Question everything
Unconventionality
8 Capricorn Moon
Composure
Responsibility
Growth without closure
9 Aquarius Neptune
Spirituality
Divine thinking
Creativity
10 Aquarius Uranus
Vast personal freedom
A shifting reality
Shattering of illusion
10 Aquarius Mercury

Comedy
The metaphysical
Communicating freely
10 Aquarius Sun
Individuality
Power to the people
Opposition to authority
11 Pisces Venus
The hopeless romantic
Sensitive
Idealistic
11 Pisces Jupiter
Healing
Empathy
Expansive feeling
12 Aries Saturn
Balancing chaos and discipline

15-05-1997

1 Gemini Ascendant
Deflection by way of comedy
The mask worn
Ruler of duality
4 Virgo Moon
Healing energy
Helpful
Intellect and curiosity
4 Virgo Mars
Goal oriented
Eye for detail
Devoted
6 Sagittarius Pluto
Karmic energy
Question everything
Unconventionality
9 Capricorn Neptune
Creativity
Sheer willpower
Raw energy
10 Aquarius Uranus
Vast personal freedom
A shifting reality
Shattering of illusion
10 Aquarius Jupiter

Finding divine beauty in all forms
Artistic pursuits above all
Roses amongst thorns
11 Aries Saturn
Balancing chaos and discipline
12 Taurus Mercury
Accumulation
Ruled by senses
Materialism
12 Taurus Sun
Loyalty
Luxury
Dependebility
12 Gemini Venus
Communication
Adventure
Mental stimulation

Dark Days

White as a ghost
An elongated shadow
Red and white
Blood in the snow

TV In Black And White

Distraction/Abstraction
A live studio audience
On television show
They see what I see-
They know what we know

Frances Farmer

'The farmer's in the cell...'
'The farmer's in the cell..'
Frances Farmer Will Have Her Revenge On
Seattle
Frances Farmer will raise hell
You bore me
I miss the comfort in misery
I'm clean now, I've never been as clean
Contemplating God aged fifteen

Frances Farmer Will Have Her Revenge On
Seattle
Frances Farmer will raise hell

Yule

Palms to the earth
Feel the darkness
And slowness
Cradled by the energy...

Holly, Mistletoe, Ivy
Cedar, Bay, Rosemary

Yule II

The divine birth
The rebirth of the sun
Burnt oranges and cinammon
Life from death-
Warmth from cold
Candles red, green and gold
Illumination and restoration
The wheel turns; the power burns.

www.ingramcontent.com/pod-product-compliance
Lightning Source LLC
La Vergne TN
LVHW050311200726
843509LV00015B/3281